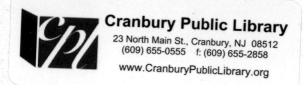

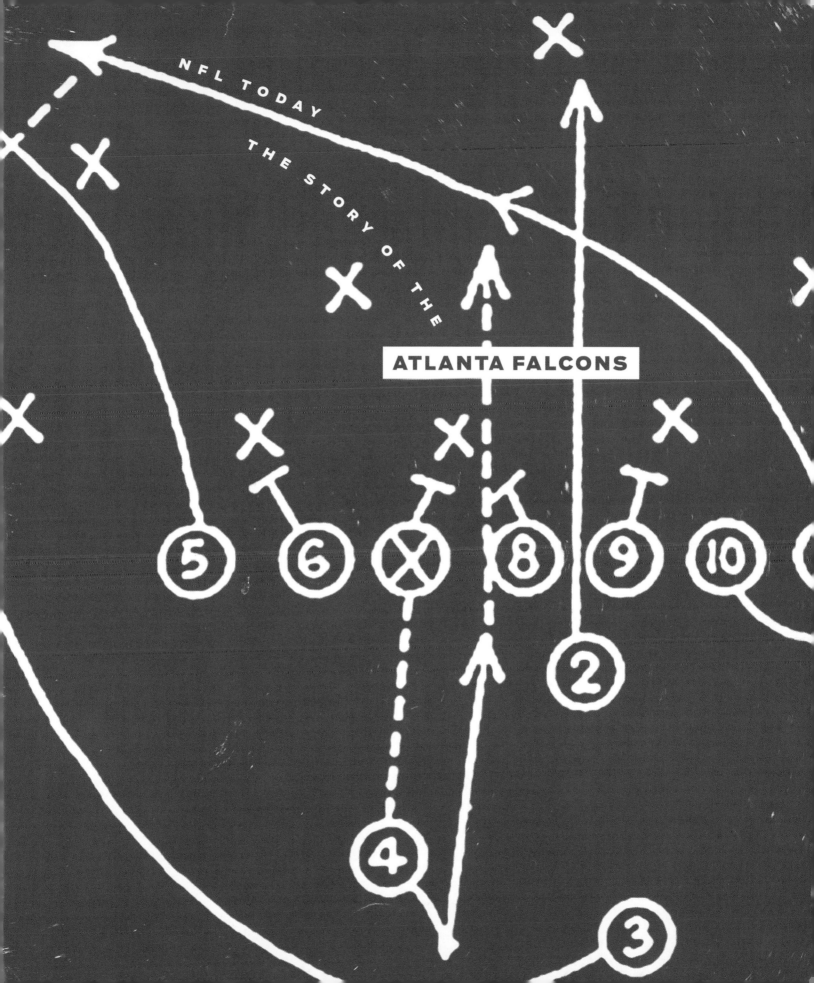

NFL TODAY

THE STORY OF THE

ATLANTA FALCONS

NFL TODAY

THE STORY OF THE ATLANTA FALCONS

NATE FRISCH

CREATIVE EDUCATION

PUBLISHED BY CREATIVE EDUCATION
P.O. BOX 227, MANKATO, MINNESOTA 56002
CREATIVE EDUCATION IS AN IMPRINT OF THE CREATIVE COMPANY
WWW.THECREATIVECOMPANY.US

DESIGN AND PRODUCTION BY BLUE DESIGN
ART DIRECTION BY RITA MARSHALL
PRINTED IN THE UNITED STATES OF AMERICA

PHOTOGRAPHS BY GETTY IMAGES (DOUG BENC, JOHN
BIEVER/SPORTS ILLUSTRATED, SCOTT BOEHM, KEVIN
C. COX, SCOTT CUNNINGHAM, GEORGE GOJKOVICH,
DREW HALLOWELL, JEFF HAYNES/AFP, ANDY HAYT,
JOHN IACONO/SPORTS ILLUSTRATED, HISHAM
IBRAHIM, PAUL JASIENSKI, CRAIG JONES/ALLSPORT,
MITCHELL LAYTON, STREETER LECKA, RONALD
C. MODRA/SPORTS IMAGERY, NFL, ERIK PEREL/
ALLSPORT, TONY RANZE/AFP, JOE ROBBINS, GEORGE
ROSE, MANNY RUBIO/NFL, STEVE SCHAEFER/AFP,
GREG TROTT/NFL, BOB VERLIN)

LIBRARY OF CONGRESS CATALOGING-IN-PUBLICATION DATA
FRISCH, NATE.
THE STORY OF THE ATLANTA FALCONS / BY NATE FRISCH.
P. CM. — (NFL TODAY)
INCLUDES INDEX.
SUMMARY: THE HISTORY OF THE NATIONAL FOOTBALL LEAGUE'S
ATLANTA FALCONS, SURVEYING THE FRANCHISE'S BIGGEST STARS
AND MOST MEMORABLE MOMENTS FROM ITS INAUGURAL SEASON
IN 1966 TO TODAY.
ISBN 978-1-60818-293-0
1. ATLANTA FALCONS (FOOTBALL TEAM)—HISTORY—JUVENILE
LITERATURE. I. TITLE.

GV956.A85F75 2013
796.332'6409758231—DC23   2012027137

FIRST EDITION
9 8 7 6 5 4 3 2 1

COVER: QUARTERBACK MATT RYAN
PAGE 2: LINEBACKERS WILLIAM MOORE, CURTIS LOFTON, AND
SEAN WEATHERSPOON
PAGE 5: WIDE RECEIVER BILLY JOHNSON
PAGE 6: WIDE RECEIVER MICHAEL JENKINS

TABLE OF CONTENTS

SIDELINE STORIES

MEET THE FALCONS

SITUATED IN THE WARM SOUTHEAST, ATLANTA IS NICKNAMED "HOTLANTA"

Nobis and the First Falcons

Looking at Atlanta, Georgia, today, it's hard to imagine that when it was incorporated in 1845, the city was little more than a stopping point where two railroads merged. But its importance as a transportation center made it grow quickly. By the start of the Civil War, the city and the services it provided were significant enough that Union soldiers burned Atlanta to the ground as a means of crippling the Confederacy. But the city rebuilt after the war, and today it remains a hub of activity, featuring the world's busiest airport and an impressive rapid transit system. Atlanta is also the headquarters of some of the most successful businesses in the world, including Coca-Cola and Turner Broadcasting.

Like the city of Atlanta, professional football was a rapidly growing enterprise in 1965. Interest piqued as the National Football League (NFL) and the upstart American Football League (AFL) competed for fans. Up to that point, however, neither league had

QUARTERBACK BOB LEE CUT HIS TEETH WITH THE VIKINGS BUT HAD BRIEF SUCCESS IN ATLANTA

Tommy Nobis

LINEBACKER / FALCONS SEASONS: 1966–76 / HEIGHT: 6-FOOT-2 / WEIGHT: 237 POUNDS

Falcons team officials never had any question about which player the club should make its first-ever draft pick in 1966. Instead, the question was if Atlanta would be able to outmaneuver the Houston Oilers of the AFL to sign All-American linebacker Tommy Nobis of the University of Texas. Quick and aggressive, Nobis was the type of player a team could build its defense around—especially a young team such as the Falcons. Atlanta outbid Houston for Nobis and never regretted the decision, as he was named Defensive Rookie of the Year in 1966 and became the team's first Pro Bowl participant that year. Nobis played 11 years in Atlanta and was selected to the Pro Bowl in 5 of those seasons. He was later named to the NFL's "All-1960s" team. Nobis once explained his no-nonsense work ethic by saying, "A man ought to have enough pride to play every game as hard as he can, wringing every bit of energy he has in him trying to win. That's the only thing that matters in football."

DEFENSIVE END CLAUDE HUMPHREY EMERGED AS A FEARSOME PASS RUSHER

any teams in the Southeast. Both leagues were keen to start up a franchise in Atlanta, but prospective owner Rankin Smith chose to join the more established NFL. The new team's name was submitted as part of a contest by a local schoolteacher, who explained that "the falcon is proud and dignified, with great courage and fight."

Before playing their first season in 1966, the Falcons were given the first overall selection in that year's NFL Draft. They wisely selected hard-nosed linebacker Tommy Nobis out of the University of Texas. Nobis always seemed to find a way to get to opposing ballcarriers. And when he found them, they stopped. "I hit 'em right in the goozle—high and hard," he explained. "That way they don't go anywhere but down." Although many league statistics were not officially recorded in 1966, some unofficial counts indicate that this human wrecking ball amassed a mind-boggling 294 tackles his rookie year.

Nobis almost singlehandedly made the team's defense respectable, but the rest of Atlanta's expansion roster was an underwhelming mix of veteran castoffs and unpolished youngsters. Atlanta's kicker literally missed the ball on the team's first ever kickoff. As the offensive squad—led by rookie quarterback Randy Johnson—struggled all season, the Falcons finished their first year near the bottom of the NFL's East Division with a 3–11 record.

After the club went an embarrassing 1–12–1 its second year, the Falcons changed coaches and drafted another defensive star. The new coach was former NFL quarterback Norm Van Brocklin. The new defensive standout was end Claude Humphrey out of Tennessee State University. Humphrey immediately keyed a fierce Falcons pass rush and was named the NFL's Defensive Rookie of the Year in 1968.

Van Brocklin was a demanding and stubborn coach, and he had a stormy relationship with many of his players. Yet, little by little, the players adapted to his coaching methods, and the team's performance improved. Led by Humphrey, linebacker Tommy Nobis, end John Zook, and cornerback Ken Reaves, the defense battered opponents. In 1969, the Falcons finished 6–8. In 1970, the NFL and AFL merged into one league, and the Falcons were placed in the National Football Conference (NFC) West Division. A year later, Atlanta recorded its first winning season (7–6–1). Still, the team's offense continued to sputter, and Van Brocklin's Falcons never became big winners.

Late in the 1974 season, Van Brocklin was fired and replaced by defensive coordinator Marion Campbell. Campbell, who had built the Atlanta defense, knew the club needed a new leader on offense, too. Scouts for the team believed they knew just the man for the job: University of California quarterback Steve Bartkowski. The Falcons engineered a trade to gain the top pick in the 1975 NFL Draft, which they used to select Bartkowski.

Atlanta fans gave the blond Californian a warm welcome, and Bartkowski loved the attention. "I enjoyed picking up the paper and reading that I was the team's savior," he later said. "I really thought I could walk in here and turn the team around overnight." However, injuries and mistakes slowed Bartkowski's rise to stardom, as did his tendency to party late into the night. He had trouble adjusting to pro defenses and suffered through a 4–10 rookie season. Then he missed much of the following two seasons with knee injuries. In 1978, Bartkowski returned healthy, but miserable preseason performances

The 1,000th Yard

The goal of every NFL running back is to rush for 1,000 yards in a season, but doing so requires hard work and a little bit of luck. In the final game of the 1972 season, Falcons halfback Dave Hampton was closing in on the 1,000-yard mark. Then, a hard run up the middle brought his total to exactly 1,000. The game was stopped, and officials presented Hampton with the game ball. Unfortunately, Hampton decided to try one more run. This time, he was thrown for a 5-yard loss, dropping his total to 995 as the game ended. Hampton kept the game ball but lost the record. The next season, Hampton also came tantalizingly close, finishing the year with 997 yards. Two years later, Hampton went into the last game of the season only 59 yards shy of 1,000. He reached the elusive total late in the game on an off-tackle run that brought his total to 1,002 yards. This time, Hampton didn't push his luck. He willingly sat out the rest of the game and took his place in the Falcons' record book.

DAVE HAMPTON ENDED HIS FALCONS CAREER WITH 3,482 RUSHING YARDS

Steve Bartkowski

QUARTERBACK / FALCONS SEASONS: 1975–85 / HEIGHT: 6-FOOT-4 / WEIGHT: 213 POUNDS

For their first nine seasons, the Falcons were known for their hard-hitting defense and their anemic offense. To turn that trend around, the club made Steve Bartkowski the number-one overall pick in the 1975 NFL Draft. Blessed with confidence and a rocket arm, the tall Californian quickly established himself as the team's leader. "The guys just seem to flock around him, and he responds," said coach Marion Campbell. "He provides the spark this team needs to win. Steve's not the tough-guy type. He's more liable to say, 'Just give me one more second, guys, and I'll get that pass in there.' They believe he can do it, so they give him that one more second." Bartkowski was named NFL Rookie of the Year by *Pro Football Weekly* in 1975, beating out future Hall-of-Famers Randy White of the Dallas Cowboys and Walter Payton of the Chicago Bears. Over his 11-year career in Atlanta, Bartkowski went to 2 Pro Bowls and led the NFL in touchdown passes once—in 1980, when he piloted Atlanta to its first NFC West title.

The Pole Bowl

Atlanta fans received an early Christmas present on December 24, 1978, when the Falcons took on the Philadelphia Eagles in Atlanta-Fulton County Stadium in their first-ever playoff game. The fans, who had been eagerly anticipating a Falcons postseason game since 1966, cheered excitedly in the rainy, 40-degree weather. The crowd quieted down considerably in the third quarter when Philadelphia moved out to a 13–0 lead, but it perked up again as quarterback Steve Bartkowski led the Falcons on a fourth-quarter charge. Bartkowski completed touchdown passes to tight end Jim Mitchell and wide receiver Wallace Francis in the last five minutes to engineer a 14–13 Atlanta victory. As the gun sounded to end the game, thousands of fans poured onto the field, mobbing the players and tearing down the goalposts. Because of the wild celebration, the game became known as "The Pole Bowl." Falcons linebacker Greg Brezina, who was in the middle of the mob, said, "Those fans hit me harder than the Eagles did. But they deserved to be on the field. They've waited 13 years for this."

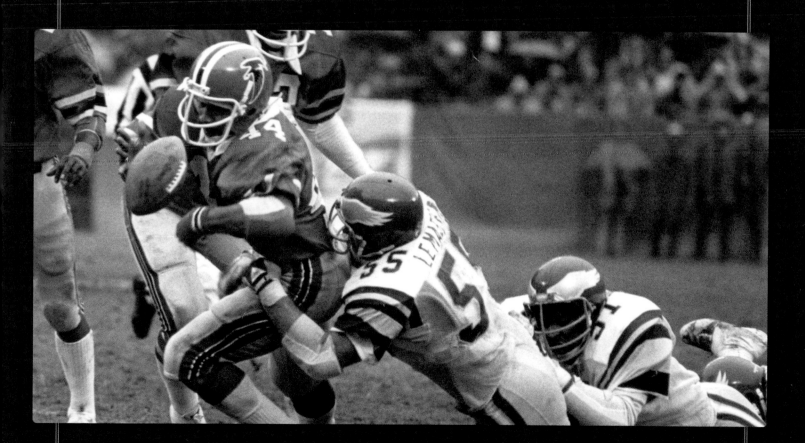

FULLBACK BUBBA BEAN AND HIS TEAMMATES MADE 1978 A YEAR TO REMEMBER

led new coach Leeman Bennett to bench the young quarterback. "That was the lowest I've ever been in my life," Bartkowski later recalled, "and it was also the best thing that ever happened to me."

Bartkowski gave up partying and refocused his life. He regained the starting position early in the 1978 season and—with the help of receivers Wallace Francis and Alfred Jenkins—led the team to a five-game winning streak. The Falcons finished 9–7 and made the playoffs for the first time in their history. After Atlanta beat the Philadelphia Eagles 14–13 in the first round, Falcons fans began dreaming of a Super Bowl. But the Dallas Cowboys gave them a rude awakening the following week, defeating Atlanta 27–20.

THE FALCONS OF THE 1960s AND EARLY '70s WERE KNOWN BEST FOR DEFENSE

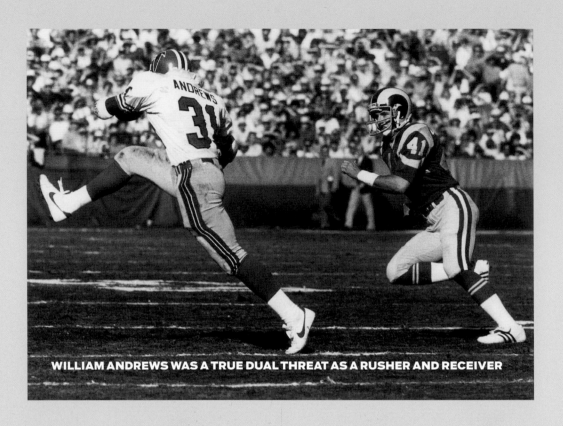

WILLIAM ANDREWS WAS A TRUE DUAL THREAT AS A RUSHER AND RECEIVER

The Exciting '80s

The Atlanta offense got a boost in 1979 with the arrival of hard-driving running back William Andrews out of Auburn University. Andrews simply overpowered tacklers as he rushed for more than 1,000 yards his rookie season. He achieved this success with a unique style, running slightly bent over with his head lowered. "I try to stay lower than my opponent," Andrews explained, "come at him in a ball, and then … POW!"

By 1980, the Falcons were ready for a run at a championship. That season, Andrews, Bartkowski, and Jenkins set new team records for rushing, passing, and pass receiving respectively. The club went 12–4 and won its first NFC West title. In the playoffs, the Falcons once again faced off against the Cowboys, this time in front of the largest crowd in Atlanta-Fulton County Stadium history. Atlanta led 27–17 in the fourth quarter, but Dallas rallied to hand the Falcons a crushing 30–27 defeat.

ATLANTA BUTTED HEADS WITH DALLAS IN EACH OF ITS FIRST TWO POSTSEASONS

William Andrews

RUNNING BACK / FALCONS SEASONS: 1979–86 / HEIGHT: 6 FEET / WEIGHT: 210 POUNDS

In his first five seasons in the NFL (1979–83), William Andrews was the best all-around running back in the league. He was named to the Pro Bowl four of those years and quickly became the Falcons' all-time leading rusher. Andrews was also an excellent receiver, and he twice gained more than 2,000 total (rushing and receiving) yards in a year. Andrews's strength and balance made it almost impossible for a single defender to bring him down. Hall of Fame safety Ronnie Lott of the San Francisco 49ers, a notoriously vicious hitter, described one attempt he made to tackle Andrews: "I ran 10 yards straight at him, as hard as I could," Lott told a *Sports Illustrated* writer. "Then boom. I slid off of him like butter. I hit the ground, and he didn't go down. I was thinking, 'What happened?'" What finally did stop Andrews was a terrible knee injury in 1984 that cut short his career. In 2004, Andrews was honored with induction into the Falcons' Ring of Honor in the Georgia Dome, a tribute to retired players who made significant contributions to the team.

GERALD RIGGS'S 397 RUSHING ATTEMPTS WERE THE MOST IN THE NFL IN 1985

After beginning the decade on a high note, the Falcons slipped toward the bottom of the NFC West. While the team fell in the standings, Andrews continued to rise, making the Pro Bowl four years in a row from 1980 to 1983. Then, in a preseason scrimmage in August 1984, Andrews got his legs tangled with another player, and he tore ligaments in his knee. The devastating injury put him on the sidelines for two seasons. Andrews tried to make a comeback in 1986, but the damaged knee wasn't strong enough for him to keep playing. Luckily for the team, Andrews's backup, bruising running back Gerald Riggs, stepped into the starting role and went on to surpass Andrews in the Falcons' record books by averaging nearly 1,000 rushing yards per season from 1982 to 1988.

Another Atlanta favorite in the 1980s was wide receiver and kick returner Billy "White Shoes" Johnson, who was known for his lightning speed and fancy footwear. Opponents hated watching those white cleats race by in a blur when Johnson returned punts and kickoffs for the Falcons. They also hated the dance he would do in the end zone to celebrate any touchdown he scored.

Big Wins with Big Ben

In 1991, the Falcons made comeback after comeback to record their first winning season in nine years. The most exciting Atlanta victory, a 17–14 last-second triumph over San Francisco, came via a trick play the team hadn't used successfully for 13 years. It was called "Big Ben Right," a variation of what is sometimes called a "Hail Mary" pass. To execute the play, several receivers race toward the end zone, and the quarterback throws the ball as far as he can. Receivers and defenders battle for the ball on what is usually a game-deciding play. In 1978, quarterback Steve Bartkowski won two games for the Falcons with Big Ben Right passes. Those two victories helped the Falcons reach the playoffs for the first time in their history. In the 1991 game against San Francisco, backup quarterback Billy Joe Tolliver (pictured) executed Big Ben Right perfectly for a 44-yard, game-winning pass to receiver Michael Haynes. Because both Atlanta and San Francisco had finished the season with identical 10–6 records, the win enabled the Falcons to beat out the 49ers for a playoff berth.

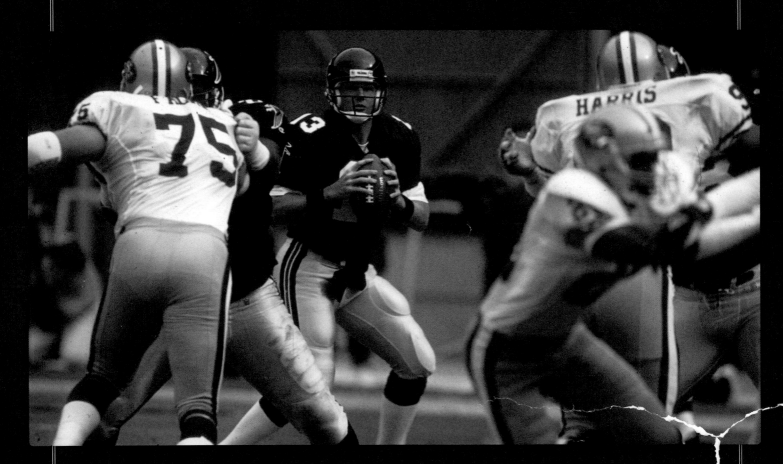

BILLY JOE TOLLIVER ENJOYED A HIGHLIGHT WITH HIS "BIG BEN" CONNECTION

"Come at him in a ball, and then ... POW!"

WILLIAM ANDREWS

Despite the presence of such stars, the Falcons continued to post losing records for the rest of the '80s. Then, late in the decade, they began rebuilding around two key draft picks: quarterback Chris Miller from the University of Oregon and cornerback Deion Sanders from Florida State University. Specializing in long downfield bombs, Miller combined with receivers Andre Rison and Michael Haynes to give the Falcons one of the most fearsome passing attacks in the league. Meanwhile, Sanders quickly became famous for shutting down opposing receivers with his blanket coverage.

The Falcons faced a challenge in signing Sanders, whose flashy moves as a cornerback and kick returner had earned him the nicknames "Neon Deion" and "Prime Time." The versatile athlete was also a top baseball player for the New York Yankees. Both franchises wanted Sanders's full-time services, but he had a different plan in mind. Sanders figured he could play both sports—baseball in the summer and football in the fall.

Sanders put his plan into action in 1989. He played baseball most of the summer for the Yankees and then reported to Falcons training camp two days before the season opener. Even without much practice, Prime Time was electric in his first Falcons game, breaking tackles and outrunning opponents on a 68-yard punt return for a touchdown. Atlanta fans were delirious with excitement, and even coach Marion Campbell was impressed. "In my 27 years in the league, I've never experienced the buzz that goes through a stadium as when this guy gets near the football," he said.

JERRY GLANVILLE WAS ONE OF FOOTBALL'S MOST COLORFUL CHARACTERS

The Falcons opened the 1990s displaying the talents of young stars such as Miller, Sanders, and Rison. They also had an eccentric new coach in Jerry Glanville. Glanville was brought in to shake things up in Atlanta, and he delivered. First, he changed the team's jerseys from red to black. Then he changed the club's attitude, installing a high-powered "Red Gun" passing offense developed by assistant coach June Jones—a former Falcons quarterback—and building an aggressive defense around linebacker Jessie Tuggle.

In 1991, the team adopted hip-hop star MC Hammer's "2 Legit 2 Quit" as its rallying cry. Taking a cue from the song, the Falcons wouldn't quit all season. They staged several exciting comebacks and stormed into the playoffs with a 10–6 record. Then they topped off the season by earning a dramatic comeback in a first-round playoff game against the New Orleans Saints. In that game, Miller connected with Haynes for a 61-yard touchdown strike that turned a late-game deficit into a 27–20 Atlanta victory. It was the Falcons' first playoff win in 13 years. Although the Falcons were eliminated from the postseason the following week by the eventual Super Bowl champion Washington Redskins, Glanville's team woke up Atlanta fans.

Dancing the Dirty Bird

Falcons players and fans had a lot to celebrate in 1998—the year Atlanta reached the Super Bowl—but no one celebrated more flamboyantly than running back Jamal Anderson. It was not only his running and pass catching but also his dancing that enabled Anderson to make team history that year. Each time he scored a touchdown (which happened 16 times during the regular season and 3 more times in the playoffs), Anderson would perform a dance he called the "Dirty Bird." Soon, fans began doing the dance in the stands after Atlanta touchdowns, and coach Dan Reeves even performed it on the field in Minnesota after the Falcons defeated the Vikings in the NFC title game. How does one do the Dirty Bird? First, you lift your right arm in the air, then bring the arm down across your chest to form a wing. Then do the same actions with your left arm. Next, flap your arms as if you're trying to fly. "Then you do whatever you feel like," said Anderson. Doing the Dirty Bird, the Falcons flew high in 1998.

JEFF GEORGE SUITED UP FOR FIVE DIFFERENT NFL TEAMS DURING HIS CAREER

Into the Dome

The next season, the Falcons moved into a new home: Atlanta's giant Georgia Dome. Playing before record-breaking home crowds, the Falcons stumbled to two straight 6–10 seasons before Glanville was fired and replaced by June Jones. Jones designed a new offense around the passing combination of strong-armed quarterback Jeff George and small but sure-handed wide receiver Terance Mathis. This pairing resulted in a team record, as Mathis caught 111 passes in 1994.

Optimism ran high in Atlanta in 1995, especially when the team got off to a 5–2 start. Led by George, Mathis, and running back Craig "Ironhead" Heyward (known for his habit of charging forward with his head down like a battering ram), the team's offense was outstanding. George became the first Atlanta quarterback to top the prestigious 4,000-yard mark in passing, while Heyward gained 1,083 yards on the ground. Despite fading in the second half of the season, the Falcons made the playoffs with a 9–7 record, only to lose in the opening round to the Green Bay Packers.

AT 260 POUNDS, CRAIG "IRONHEAD" HEYWARD WAS A LOAD TO BRING DOWN

Deion Sanders

CORNERBACK / FALCONS SEASONS: 1989–93 / HEIGHT: 6-FOOT-1 / WEIGHT: 198 POUNDS

When Deion Sanders was on the football field, opposing quarterbacks avoided throwing in his direction. That was because the receiver Sanders was covering was almost never going to be open for a pass. Perhaps no cornerback in NFL history blanketed his man as effectively as the lightning-quick Sanders did. But covering pass receivers was only part of what the multitalented star could do on a football field. During some games, Sanders joined the offense, too, and he caught 60 career passes. He was even more dangerous as a kick returner, returning a total of six punts and three kickoffs for touchdowns throughout his career. In 2000, he was selected by Pro Football Hall of Fame voters as the punt returner on the NFL's All-Time Team. Football was not the only sport in which Sanders excelled, though. He played major league baseball for nine seasons, leading the National League in triples in 1992 and twice finishing second in stolen bases. "Prime Time" is the only athlete ever to have hit a major-league home run and to have scored an NFL touchdown in the same week.

PLAYING IN THE ROWDY GEORGIA DOME, THE LATE-'90s FALCONS FLEW HIGH

Fortunately for Atlanta fans, the Falcons were about to get serious about a postseason run. In January 1997, the team replaced Jones with Dan Reeves, who had previously coached the Denver Broncos to three Super Bowl appearances in the 1980s. Reeves's hiring excited both Atlanta fans and players. "He's a winner," said Falcons defensive end Chuck Smith, "and he knows what it takes to get it done in this league."

One of Coach Reeves's first moves was to acquire veteran quarterback Chris Chandler from the Houston Oilers to provide much-needed experience and leadership. Chandler combined with running back Jamal Anderson and wide receiver Bert Emanuel to establish a smooth-running offense in Atlanta. But in 1997, the Falcons' defensive line made an even more remarkable turnaround, as it set a club record for quarterback sacks with 55 and often kept opposing passers feeling nervous in the pocket. Such achievements left the Falcons and their fans brimming with confidence.

The patience of Falcons fans was finally rewarded in 1998 as the club romped to a 14–2 record and

the top spot in the NFC West. Behind Anderson's strong running and Chandler's pinpoint passing, the Falcons' offense pounded opposing defenses. Anderson also set an NFL record with 410 carries and a club record with 1,846 rushing yards. Meanwhile, the defense, led by Tuggle and fellow linebacker Cornelius Bennett, ranked near the top of the NFC.

Tuggle, who would spend 14 total seasons in Atlanta, described the magical season this way: "When we hit the field, a lot of veteran leadership took over, and we felt like we couldn't lose. Sometimes you have a team—it may not be the most talented team—but when you believe in yourself and fight for one goal and become one unit, then great things happen for you. That's what happened

ATLANTA'S 1998 RUN TOOK IT ALL THE WAY TO A CLASH WITH THE CHAMPION BRONCOS

Vick's Fall

When the Falcons made Michael Vick the top overall pick in the 2001 NFL Draft, they knew they were getting a player who could do spectacular things on the field but could sometimes be a little out of control in his personal life. What they didn't know was that Vick had a dark secret: Vick and some friends had organized an illegal dogfighting and gambling enterprise. They set up a kennel on Vick's sprawling Virginia estate, where they trained dogs to fight and then staged vicious battles between the animals. The existence of the dogfighting ring and Vick's involvement in it became big news in the summer of 2007. After several of the quarterback's partners pleaded guilty, Vick also agreed to a plea bargain and was sentenced to 23 months in jail. With Vick imprisoned, the Falcons lost one of the most exciting players in team history. But Vick lost far more, forfeiting much of the $130-million contract he had signed with Atlanta, many lucrative endorsement contracts, and the respect of thousands of fans. Vick would bounce back as a star for the Eagles in 2010, but his fall in Atlanta was quick and costly.

THE FALCONS' EXCITING MICHAEL VICK ERA CAME TO A SHOCKING END IN 2007

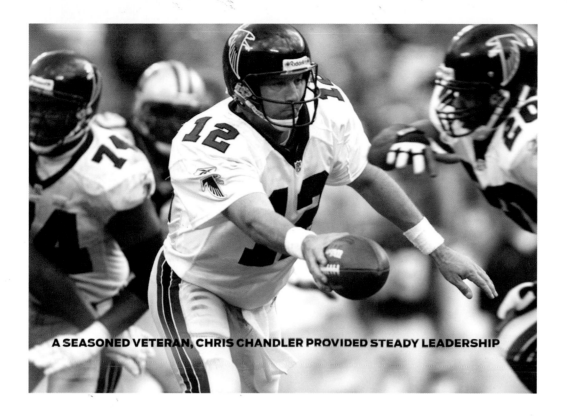

A SEASONED VETERAN, CHRIS CHANDLER PROVIDED STEADY LEADERSHIP

to us. We got a little confidence. We took that confidence and mixed in some pretty good ability, and we went a long way."

In the postseason, Atlanta edged past the San Francisco 49ers 20–18 to reach the NFC Championship Game opposite the 15–1 Minnesota Vikings. Playing in Minnesota's Metrodome, the two teams fought to a 27–27 tie in regulation and then kept battling into overtime. Atlanta's defense twice stopped the powerful Vikings offense before the Falcons won the game on a field goal by kicker Morten Andersen. The once lowly Falcons were bound for the Super Bowl at last.

In Super Bowl XXXIII against the defending world champion Denver Broncos, the Falcons took a 3–0 lead five minutes into the game. But the Atlanta defense could not contain Denver quarterback John Elway, who directed a Broncos attack that totaled more than 450 yards. The final result was a 34–19 Denver win that ended Atlanta's championship dreams.

The Falcons followed up their Super Bowl season with two disappointing years. Coach Reeves knew that the team needed new blood, so he engineered a trade with the San Diego Chargers to obtain the top pick in the 2001 NFL Draft. The Falcons used the opportunity to select Michael Vick, a multidimensional quarterback who had excelled as both a passer and a runner during his college career at Virginia Tech.

Vick's arrival signaled a new era for Atlanta. In 2002, for the first time in 10 years, all 8 of the team's home games were sellouts, as fans packed the Georgia Dome to see the new, highflying Falcons. Vick quickly blossomed into one of the NFL's most exciting stars, passing for nearly 3,000 yards and rushing

WIDE RECEIVER BRIAN FINNERAN RACKED UP 3,072 RECEIVING YARDS IN 9 YEARS

Jessie Tuggle

LINEBACKER / FALCONS SEASONS: 1987–2000 / HEIGHT: 5-FOOT-11 / WEIGHT: 231 POUNDS

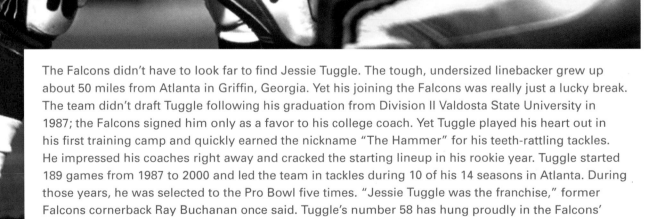

The Falcons didn't have to look far to find Jessie Tuggle. The tough, undersized linebacker grew up about 50 miles from Atlanta in Griffin, Georgia. Yet his joining the Falcons was really just a lucky break. The team didn't draft Tuggle following his graduation from Division II Valdosta State University in 1987; the Falcons signed him only as a favor to his college coach. Yet Tuggle played his heart out in his first training camp and quickly earned the nickname "The Hammer" for his teeth-rattling tackles. He impressed his coaches right away and cracked the starting lineup in his rookie year. Tuggle started 189 games from 1987 to 2000 and led the team in tackles during 10 of his 14 seasons in Atlanta. During those years, he was selected to the Pro Bowl five times. "Jessie Tuggle was the franchise," former Falcons cornerback Ray Buchanan once said. Tuggle's number 58 has hung proudly in the Falcons' Ring of Honor since 2004, and no Atlanta player has worn the number since.

for 777 more in his rookie season. Other offensive stars that year included halfback Warrick Dunn and second-year tight end Alge Crumpler. Together, they propelled Atlanta back into the postseason.

Describing Vick's play, sportswriter Mike Holbrook noted, "He has shown a penchant for doing the impossible and producing at least one play that leaves you saying, 'That's impossible,' or 'I've never seen that before.' He's the closest thing to a human highlight film as there is in the sport."

In the first round of the 2002 playoffs, Vick and the Falcons shocked football experts by handing the Green Bay Packers their first-ever playoff loss at Lambeau Field in wintry Wisconsin. However, they fell to the Philadelphia Eagles the next week, delaying their hopes of a return to football's biggest stage.

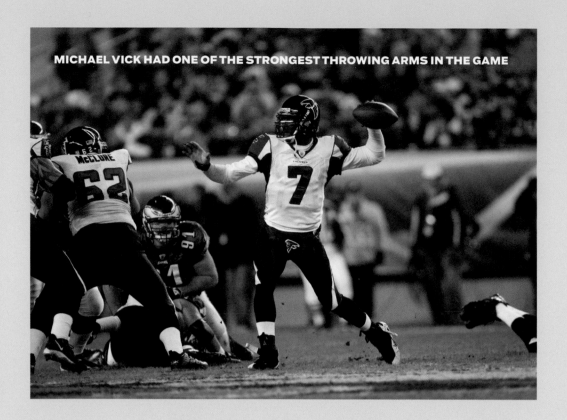

MICHAEL VICK HAD ONE OF THE STRONGEST THROWING ARMS IN THE GAME

From Michael to Matty

The Falcons found themselves in a hole before the season even began in 2003 when, in a preseason game, Vick suffered a broken leg that would keep him sidelined most of the year. Vick tried to make the most of the limited time he had upon his return, helping the Falcons win three of their final four games, including one victory in which he rushed for 141 yards. But it was too little, too late, and after Atlanta finished with a 5–11 record, Coach Reeves was dismissed and replaced by Jim Mora Jr.

Mora still had faith in the offensive trio of Vick, Dunn, and Crumpler, while rock-steady linebacker Keith Brooking, relentless lineman Patrick Kearney, and rookie cornerback DeAngelo Hall anchored the defense. The club reversed its previous year's showing by going 11–5 to finish atop the recently formed NFC South. After a first-round bye in the playoffs, the Falcons offense ran wild in round two, running up 47 points in a victory over the St. Louis Rams, but it then managed only 10 points in a loss to the Eagles in the NFC Championship Game. Still, the Falcons looked to the future with optimism.

KEITH BROOKING REPRESENTED THE FALCONS IN THE PRO BOWL FIVE TIMES

ATLANTA MADE THE PLAYOFFS IN FOUR OF FIVE SEASONS UNDER MIKE SMITH

"I can look in my teammates' eyes and tell that we're not fully satisfied," said Brooking. "There is still a hunger inside of us, and that's what's so great about this team."

Brooking's words rang true during the first half of the 2005 season when the Falcons got off to a 6–2 start. However, a shaky second half capped off by three straight losses ended Atlanta's season at 8–8 and out of the playoffs. The following 7–9 year continued the disappointment. But the most deflating news of all came after that season.

ick was arrested during the summer of 2007 and imprisoned for his involvement in a secretive dogfighting operation. With the face of the franchise no longer in the picture, the Falcons went from mediocre to terrible, finishing 4–12 in 2007. Toward the end of the season, Atlanta—determined to establish a different identity— installed Mike Smith as its new head coach.

Reinforcements came quickly. In 2008, the Falcons added rookie quarterback Matt Ryan and barrel-chested running back Michael Turner. These newcomers sparked the offense, while standout pass rusher John Abraham led the defense. The new-look Falcons soared to an 11–5 record and earned a playoff berth. But against the Arizona Cardinals, the team's stars struggled. Ryan committed 3 turnovers, Turner was held to 42 rushing yards, and Abraham tallied just 2 tackles in a 30–24 defeat.

Following the loss, team officials wondered if their offense was too young. That off-season, Atlanta

A Grand Unveiling

By the late 2000s, the Falcons had the dubious distinction of never having posted consecutive winning seasons—despite having played for more than four decades. The 2007 season was another one of their low points, as the Falcons posted an embarrassing 4–12 record. Determined to make long-term improvements, Atlanta acquired former Chargers running back Michael Turner, who had shown promise but was used sparingly in San Diego. The Falcons then selected quarterback Matt Ryan with the third pick of the 2008 NFL Draft. Atlanta fans had high hopes for the new additions, but going into the 2008 season, the two players were still relatively unproven commodities. In Week 1 against the Detroit Lions, the duo quickly squashed any lingering doubts. Ryan completed his very first pass attempt for a 62-yard touchdown and completed nearly 70 percent of his passes. Not to be outdone, Turner rambled for 220 yards—including a 66-yard dash—setting the franchise single-game record for rushing yards. These coming-out performances jumpstarted what turned out to be an impressive 11–5 season. They also represented the beginning of a potent backfield pairing that led Atlanta to four straight winning seasons by 2012.

MATT RYAN AND MICHAEL TURNER TOOK THE OFFENSE IN ATLANTA TO A NEW LEVEL

BOTH POWERFUL AND SHIFTY, MICHAEL TURNER HAD A NOSE FOR THE END ZONE

THE FALCONS EMERGED AS AN NFC SOUTH CONTENDER IN 2008

added veteran Tony Gonzalez, the most prolific pass-catching tight end in NFL history. The Falcons burst out of the gate in 2009, winning four of their first five games. Unfortunately, they sputtered in midseason, due in part to the absence of an injured Turner. The Falcons finished the season with three straight wins, but their 9–7 record was not good enough for a postseason berth.

The Falcons rebounded in 2010. Ryan, Turner, and Gonzalez all enjoyed Pro Bowl seasons, as did field-stretching receiver Roddy White. The star-studded offense led Atlanta to an NFC-best 13–3 record and a first-round bye in the playoffs. A Super Bowl return seemed within reach. However, against the red-hot Packers, the Falcons experienced a case of postseason déjà vu as Ryan committed 3 turnovers and Turner ran for just 39 yards. Atlanta's remarkable season went up in flames as Green Bay torched it 48–21.

Although 2011 started with a meager 2–3 record in Atlanta, pieces started falling into place as the season unfolded. Big and speedy rookie wideout Julio Jones added a deep threat to the already potent Atlanta offense, and emerging outside linebacker Sean Weatherspoon anchored the defense, which was among the league's best against the run. The Falcons finished with a solid 10–6 mark and a return to postseason play. Unfortunately for the Atlanta faithful, the Falcons fizzled in the playoffs. Facing the streaking (and eventual Super Bowl champion) New York Giants, Atlanta was smashed 24–2. "That shouldn't happen to a team like we have," said Gonzalez. "We're a lot better than this."

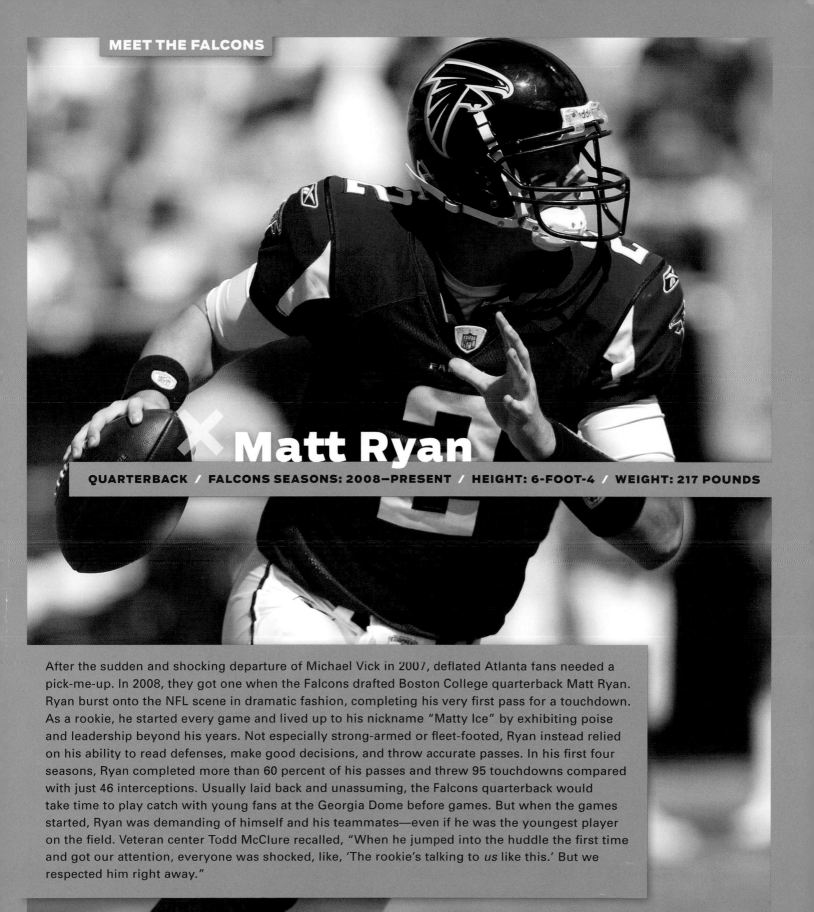

Matt Ryan

QUARTERBACK / FALCONS SEASONS: 2008–PRESENT / HEIGHT: 6-FOOT-4 / WEIGHT: 217 POUNDS

After the sudden and shocking departure of Michael Vick in 2007, deflated Atlanta fans needed a pick-me-up. In 2008, they got one when the Falcons drafted Boston College quarterback Matt Ryan. Ryan burst onto the NFL scene in dramatic fashion, completing his very first pass for a touchdown. As a rookie, he started every game and lived up to his nickname "Matty Ice" by exhibiting poise and leadership beyond his years. Not especially strong-armed or fleet-footed, Ryan instead relied on his ability to read defenses, make good decisions, and throw accurate passes. In his first four seasons, Ryan completed more than 60 percent of his passes and threw 95 touchdowns compared with just 46 interceptions. Usually laid back and unassuming, the Falcons quarterback would take time to play catch with young fans at the Georgia Dome before games. But when the games started, Ryan was demanding of himself and his teammates—even if he was the youngest player on the field. Veteran center Todd McClure recalled, "When he jumped into the huddle the first time and got our attention, everyone was shocked, like, 'The rookie's talking to *us* like this.' But we respected him right away."

VETERAN END JOHN ABRAHAM (#55) CONTINUED TO LEAD THE DEFENSE IN 2012

JULIO JONES PROVIDED A BIG, FAST PASSING TARGET FOR MATT RYAN

Gonzalez's words proved almost prophetic in the 2012 season. The Falcons roared through the regular season with an NFC-best 13–3 record. However, many members of the media—noting Atlanta's dismal recent playoff history—predicted that the Seahawks would win in the divisional round of the playoffs. Such skepticism perhaps fueled the Falcons, who led 20–0 by halftime of that game. When Seattle roared back, scoring a touchdown for a 28–27 edge with 31 seconds remaining, the Atlanta faithful were rattled. Ryan coolly saved the day, though, completing two passes to set up kicker Matt Bryant's game-winning field goal.

Hosting San Francisco in the NFC title game, the Falcons bolted out to an early 17–0 lead. But the 49ers' aggressive defense held Atlanta scoreless in the second half, and San Francisco overtook the Falcons midway through the final quarter. There would be no miracle comeback this time as the Falcons fell one game short of the Super Bowl.

For going on five decades, the Atlanta Falcons have often toyed with the emotions of their fans. Like the bird for which they are named, Altanta's Falcons have shown a tendency for sudden, diving descents. But, like the city of Atlanta, the franchise has also demonstrated a knack for strong comebacks. What happens next is anyone's guess, but with the Falcons in the midst of their most successful era in team history, they are hopeful their next move will be to the top of the NFL.

INDEX